Choosing the right Collection Agency for your Business

By Michelle Dunn

Also available for Kindle

Table of Contents

Introduction

With all the bad press about collection agencies how do you decide which one to use or if you should use one at all? This short book will help business owners make an educated decision about which collection agency they want representing their business and the most efficient ways to work with an agency to get the best return.

I will also talk about the red flags that can tell you that you need a collection agency, signs to look for, what to expect and how using a collection agency can affect your business. Failing to have a collection agency hired and ready to collect on your past due accounts before it is needed is the biggest mistake business owners make in collections.

This short little book is critical for anyone who needs to hire a collection agency but doesn't know how to do it or what to look for.

How to choose the right Collection Agency for your Business

When you start thinking about hiring a collection agency, you are probably like every other business owner out there wondering what to look for and how to choose the best agency.   When you look up collection agencies online or in your local phone book there are some things you should look for.

You want to try and find a collection agency that is familiar with your specific business. If you are a medical office, an agency that collects on student debts won't do you much good. An agency that is familiar with your type of customers and debt will know better questions to ask and solutions to offer based on that industry.

For example, I was once a credit manager for an oil company, doing collections for an oil company, the questions I might ask a past due customer would differ from the questions you would need to ask when collecting on past due credit card debt or an auto loan. Ask other people in your industry who they use for a collection agency to get an idea of what your options are.

Choose an agency based on your customers, are your customers' consumers or other businesses – most collection agencies specialize in either consumer or commercial debt collections.

Does the agency belong to any trade associations, a local chamber of commerce or rotary club? This gives them credibility and you can call them for a reference on the agency. Also check the Better Business

Bureau website for a history and to see if there are any complaints against the agency.

With all the horror stories out there about abusive debt collectors, you want to make sure the agency you hire isn't one of them. Ask the agency about the process they use to collect a debt; will they be sensitive to an individual situation? The agency should quickly notify you if they discover a consumer who may be a hardship case and recommend a procedure to follow to help that debtor. In the new economy we are dealing with, this happens more now than it has in the last few years so it is important to be aware of it and know what you will do if it happens.

Third party collectors must comply with Federal and state laws where they are located and where the consumer that owes the money is located. By checking references you will be able to determine if the agency you are interested in has a history of breaking these laws and being sued for violations. If you find an agency like that, run away!

The laws a third party collection agency must follow are the FDCPA and the FCRA, both acts are enforced by The Federal Trade Commission. (www.FTC.gov)

As you look for a collection agency to use for your business, you may find some websites offering debt collection services that you aren't too sure about. Some of the things to keep an eye out for when you are looking for an agency are to make sure they have a physical address on their website, and not just a PO Box. Look for a phone number, email and contact information to be easily available.

See if they have any logo's to any trade associations or memberships they may have that you can contact to see if they are a member and ask how long they have been a member. Also ask if there have ever been any complaints about them.

Make sure their rates or pricing are readily available on their website, and look for testimonials from happy customers. Ask questions, now is the time to ask.

Look out for agencies that don't have a physical address or a phone number listed on their website and that also don't list that they belong to any trade associations or local networking groups.

If you don't get a live person when you call, and get a recording instead – you might want to consider that when your customers may call to make payments they will get that same recording. Don't you hate it when you call somewhere and you don't get a live person?

Make sure the agency you choose represents how you would like your customers to be treated and remember that the agency you choose is a reflection of you and your business. Make sure the agency is licensed and bonded in the states you will hire it to collect in and ask them if they have errors and omissions insurance.

If an agency has the lowest price out there, make sure to do your research. Cheaper is not always better and you do get what you pay for. No matter which agency you decide to go with get a signed contract and make sure you have a copy. Know what the agency will do for you and what your responsibilities are.

As you research collection agencies and take all of this information I have given you into consideration, here is a short list of the questions to ask when making a decision to hire a collection agency:

- Do they specialize in a specific type of debt collection – consumer/commercial, medical, retail, utilities, student debt.

- What associations or networking groups do they belong to? Are they in good standing?

- What are their collection procedures do they only send letters or send letters and call, how often do they call, can you see copies of the letters they send out?

- Have they had any or excessive complaints against them for law violations? How often, how many, when was the last time, how were they resolved?

- Do they list all contact information clearly on their website, correspondence and do they identify themselves when they answer the phone? Do you get a live person or a recording when you call? What will the debtors get when they call?

- What is the pricing structure, is it a flat monthly fee or a commission? What is the commission? Is that across the board or do I get a discount based on the volume of accounts I place with your agency? Do you disperse payments monthly? Do you send out update reports on accounts and if so, how often?

- Ask for the names and phone numbers of current customers, call them. Ask them:
  - How long have you been using this agency?
  - How has their service been so far?
  - How many accounts do you normally place with them a month?
  - What do you like the most about this agency?
  - What do dislike about them?

When to use a collection agency

Now that you have decided on a collection agency to use for your company, you have to figure out when is it time to use a collection agency? This is different for every business out there. Depending on your terms, you might place accounts for collection after 90 days or after 120 days. Some businesses place accounts with a collection agency at 65 days.

If you are going to do some in house collections before sending accounts over to an agency, you may end up sending accounts sooner than later. This is because as you work on the accounts you will become familiar with the signs to look out for that indicates when someone may be running into financial trouble and you want to make every effort to get paid.

As an account ages, the chances of collecting on that account decrease dramatically. It sometimes becomes a better use of your company's time and resources to concentrate on other aspects of your business.

When an account reaches 90 to 120 days past due, it's time to consider placing them with your collection agency. Some people place accounts at 60 days, some wait well over a year. Just remember that the sooner you place an account with a collection agency the better your chances are of getting paid. This is why some agencies will charge a higher commission on old accounts. They are very hard to collect, so keep that in mind when you decide when you want to place your accounts for collection.

I just mentioned the signs to look out for that indicate when someone may be running into financial trouble and you want to make every effort to get paid. These are the signs that you may need to place an account with a collection agency:

- A fairly new (less than a year) customer does not respond to invoices, statements or letters. For some unknown reason the customer will not or cannot pay. You can keep your losses down by placing an account like this for collection sooner than later.

- Your payment terms fail. In some cases irresponsible customers pay when and if they want to. This group is responsible for 25-50% of the cost of collections. Determine the customers who may play payment games with you and get rid of them.

- The customer is making repetitious, unfounded complaints. Make sure you have the documentation to support the debt and place them for collection. Spend your time with customers that order consistently, pay on time and deserve your attention.

- The customer starts denying responsibility for the debt. Without professional collection help, these accounts are time consuming to you and your business.

- The customer has marital difficulties. It has been my experience personally and professionally that delinquency goes along with marital problems. In this situation your best bet is to quickly place the account with an agency before the problems get worse or the disappearance of one or both of the responsible parties. People start getting separated and moving, mail starts getting returned and phone numbers change. Let an agency locate the customers and do the collection work for you to resolve the debt as quickly as possible.

- Starting a pattern of paying late, it may start slowly and then the balances owed will become later and larger.

- Frequent address and/or phone number changes.

- Frequent changes in their job, where and when they work, how much they make.

What does a Collection Agency Do?

A collection agency is a service business that helps businesses collect on accounts that are delinquent. Collectors have a vast knowledge of collection techniques, technology and compliance issues. Using a collection agency will save you time and give you better results than you might get on your own.

Collection agencies spend all day every day collecting debt. Some collectors are on the phone all day calling debtors about bills owed to their clients, trying to work with them to get the bill paid, sometimes setting up payment arrangements, or sending verification of a debt that someone is disputing.

Collection agencies also do skip tracing, this is the process of locating a debtor that has had their mail returned, maybe the phone is disconnected and they don't work at the last known job you had on file. The agency now has to locate them in order to even begin trying to collect for you. This service is normally included in the commission fee you pay the agency.

Most collection agencies also report the debts to the credit bureaus UNLESS the creditor has already reported the debt. If you report debts to the credit bureaus, make sure to let your agency know so that they don't also report it. Having the debt reported by the agency is also normally included as a service you pay for through the commission rate.

Working with a Collection Agency

Once you decide on a collection agency, they may provide you with online or printed forms to list your accounts on. In some cases you may be able to upload spreadsheets of accounts directly to them or their collection software. Give as much information as possible because having accurate information about the account will improve collections. In all cases, the minimum information should include:

- The correct, full name, address and any phone numbers and email addresses of the customer

- Name of the customers spouse, if they have one

- Let them know if the mail has been returned and for what reason

- Customer and spouses occupation or last known job and phone number

- Names of relatives, friends, neighbors and references (normally found on the credit application)

- Summary of any disputes or problems

- Date of last transaction, order or payment

- Nicknames, aliases or a maiden name if you know it

If you have had all of your customers fill out a credit application, most or all of the above information can be found on there. The summary of disputes or problems should be documented in your computer and can just be printed out or emailed with the accounts.

Cooperate with your collection agency, rely on their experience, diligence and judgment for the best and quickest results and promptly refer any contact from the customer back to the collection agency.

Don't place your accounts with more than one agency. Make sure that if you decide to change agencies that the accounts are only being worked on by one agency. Sign one contract with one agency, and if you decide to switch, check your contract to see how long it is in effect and what happens when you cancel or pull accounts from that agency before it is time to renew the contract. Make sure to pull any accounts from an agency that has had them before placing them with another agency. Also ask the agency if they reported the debt to the credit bureaus, so your new agency does not report them as well. Collection agencies fees are based on results, not on the time spent on the account. Don't expect payments to be made immediately.

When I owned my collection agency, I would have clients fax over a delinquent account to collect at 3:00 and call the next morning to ask me if I got the money. If you do things like that, no agency will want to work with you.

Expect your collection agency to send you a monthly statement showing which accounts paid, what date they paid, how much they paid, how much of that goes to the collection agency and how much you will receive. Many agencies are now offering a secure website where you can sign in and look at your accounts and see up to date information on the collection action taken and if any payments have been made. Some agencies will also send updates on accounts at other times or if requested, talk to your agency to see what they can offer you.

Once you start using a collection agency you will be excited to have taken care of all the bad debt floating around your receivables and anxious to see results.

Having been a credit manager using collection agencies and having been an agency owner I want to tell you what not to do so that you can have a successful working relationship with your collection agency.

Don't call weekly for updates, ask if they can send updates or if they have an online option or another way you can satisfy this need for weekly updates. When you call collection agencies to ask for updates, they are spending the time they would be trying to collect your money, talking to you. Let them do their job.

Don't negotiate a payment with your customer after placing an account with a collection agency and if you do that – don't withhold the fact that the debt has been paid from the collection agency. Not only is it illegal for them to continue trying to collect on a debt that has been paid, it violates your agreement.

Let your agency know if someone pays you directly so they can report the debt as paid to the credit bureaus and close it off their books, they will charge you the commission on your next statement.

I said this before but don't place your accounts with more than one agency. No one wins in that situation. It is illegal, it is unethical and you won't get paid.

How collection agencies get paid

Most collection agencies charge a commission or percentage based on the many factors of the accounts they are trying to collect. Some agencies charge a flat monthly fee and some charge per letter or call.

If an agency charges a commission, it will normally be a percentage for "standard" accounts. That would be any accounts that are maybe 60 days old, have a good address and phone number and the debt is pretty collectible. When I had my agency, my collection rate was 25%, if an account was under $75 or over 1 year old my commission was 50%. When I had a large client placing many accounts weekly or monthly, I would give them a special rate based on the number of accounts, how often they placed accounts, the age of the accounts and the balance due.

Some agencies will charge a flat monthly fee based on the number of accounts you place, how frequently you place them, the dollar amounts, and age. They may also charge per letter or per phone call and let you decide the frequency of each. Collection agencies may also offer other paid service, check out their websites and compare to see what the average free structure is and what works for you.

Collection Agency payments and updates

Most collection agencies send payment monthly and some may offer twice a month. Quite a few agencies even offer online updates on the payments and the status of your accounts that they are working on. You no longer have to wait a month to find out who paid, you can search online or even call for an update.

Remember that when you place accounts with a collection agency, that doesn't guarantee that the debt will be paid and the agency certainly never guarantees a time frame for it to be paid. This is why the commission pay structure works well.

Many businesses that use collection agencies write the balances off to bad debt when they place them with a collection agency. If you do this, any money the collection agency collects for you is gravy. It is money you were not expecting to receive. With this in mind give your agency some time to process and work on the account.

Agencies also have to give the debtor 30 days to request verification of the debt and/or dispute the debt by law. Keep this in mind when you are asking them for updates, remember nothing will happen normally within the first 30 days, other than requesting verification and processing the account.

How using a collection agency affects your business

Once you decide to turn your past due accounts over to a collection agency, be prepared for those customers that wouldn't return your calls, to call you. This doesn't always happen but it is very common. It has been my experience that the customer will call the business once they receive notification from the collection agency that they are handling the account. When this happens just remember to refer the customer back to the collection agency and let the agency know what contact has been made so they can follow up.

This sometimes makes a business feel uncomfortable, especially if it is a small business, so I always tell them to say it is out of their hands, that their book keeper or accountant handles that and it is policy they have to follow. Kind of push off the blame but hopefully still get paid.

Sometimes a customer will come back to you for services or products after they have paid off a collection agency. Do not extend credit to this customer if you work with them at all. Once you have placed an account with a collection agency to get paid, only accept cash payments, up front. This customer cost you money when they didn't pay their bill, if they continue to purchase from you and have to pay cash, you might recoup your losses.

As a credit grantor, you should be aware of some basic principals:

- Granting credit carries an unavoidable element of risk. You will have some losses regardless of how closely you screen applicants.
- There are some fundamental procedures that can help in your collection efforts. While no collection procedures will completely cover all your needs, there are some general ideas that can assist you, regardless of the goods or services you provide.
- A clear understanding by both parties of the terms of the credit transactions when it is initiated.
- A systematic and diligent follow up of every account.
- A periodic age analysis of every outstanding account.

Extending Credit

As a credit grantor, your business is one of many that allows consumers to use goods and services immediately and pay for them later. While extending credit increases your gross sales, it also puts you at risk of some losses due to nonpayment.

Most businesses that "write-off" a percentage of sales to bad debts have an established rate of procedure for this action. In most businesses, this rate runs from 0.5% to 1% on low-profit transactions, and up to 5% on high-profit sales and services. When the charge-off rate exceeds 5%, it becomes necessary to find ways to improve controls over bad debt losses.

You don't have to accept excessive losses as an inherent part of doing business and extending credit. The fundamentals of establishing and maintaining effective controls over bad debt are comparatively simple, and it is possible to reduce these loses.

Identifying Bad Debt

You can keep bad debts to a minimum and have more success recovering them if you identify them early. Your actions at this point of your credit-collection procedures are vital. Your reaction can mean the difference between recovery or loss. When you identify a potential bad debt, you need to act promptly and decisively. Usually the more time that passes, the less consumers pay.

Accounts that are carried indefinitely usually originate with creditors who do a limited amount of business, have the highest credit losses or the lowest debt recovery. Most national associations keep track of averages of delinquency for their industry.

Reducing Bad Debt

You should have a standard, in-house written policy on handling accounts. The policy should include when to call new customers, when to call established customers and when to send letters.

Assuming that there is regular account billing, you will find that most credit users will pay as agreed. A certain number will pay after a mild reminder. Some will encounter a change in economic situation that makes it difficult to pay, such as illness or loss of job. After a regular follow-up with these consumers, they will usually give insight into their financial situation, their reason for nonpayment, a promise to pay and eventually they will fulfill this promise. A small number of consumers, rarely over 5%, will require more attention, but will eventually pay.

These consumers are not our main concern. They are mentioned only to emphasize a simple, fundamental collection practice - keep the account good. This can usually only be achieved by giving each account proper and constant attention.

A successful in-house policy must:

- be tough yet flexible
- have specific guidelines of action
- contain self-evaluation
- be consistently enforced

Proper and consistent attention involves developing a collection schedule and following each step fully before moving on to the next step. It means that you never move backward or repeat a step in the hope of salvaging an account.

Conclusion

When to Hire a Professional Collector

As an account ages, the chances of collecting on it decrease dramatically. It's expensive to carry accounts that you will not be able to collect using the methods at your disposal. It's often a better use of your company's time and resources to concentrate on other aspects of your business.

A Professional collection service can assist you in collecting accounts that remain delinquent. Collectors have a vast knowledge of collection techniques, technology and compliance issues. Using a professional collection service will save time and likely yield better results.

To recap how to choose the right collection agency for your business:

1. Make sure the agency is licensed, bonded and insured.

2. Inquire about the fee structure and what it includes BEFORE signing a contract.

3. Always sign a contract after reading it and making sure it is to your benefit.

4. Do they train and certify their collectors?

5. How many complaints have been brought against them? Check this through memberships they hold, the Better Business Bureau website and the Federal Trade Commission for complaints about violations of HIPPA, FDCPA and FCRA.

Resources

Directory of collection agencies by state:

http://collection-agencies.regionaldirectory.us/

Michelle Dunn Online: http://www.MichelleDunn.com

Connect with Michelle on LinkedIn:
www.linkedin.com/in/creditmd/

Twitter: @DunnMich

Facebook: http://www.facebook.com/pages/The-Guide-to-Getting-Paid/175893280661?

Commercial Credit Management Association: http://ccma-llc.com/Home_Page.php

Blogs

http://www.Credit-and-Collections.com

http://steveharms-creditandcollections.blogspot.com/

http://receivableaccounts.blogspot.com/2011/12/auditing-your-collection-agency-101.html

http://www.bccs2.com/credit-and-collection-articles.php/

Groups

LinkedIn group: **The Guide to Getting Paid**

Join here: http://www.linkedin.com/groups/Guide-Getting-Paid-2652085?home

Credit and Collections Discussion group, to **Subscribe, send an email to:** creditandcollections-subscribe@yahoogroups.com

About the author

Michelle Dunn is a 26 year debt collection industry veteran, entrepreneur, award winning author, self-syndicated columnist, one of the Top 5 Women in Collections and one of the Top 50 most influential collection professionals in her industry.

Award winning author & columnist, Michelle Dunn giving an interview for NPR at the NHPR offices in Concord NH.

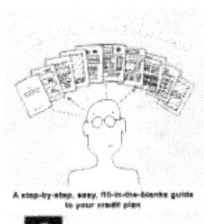

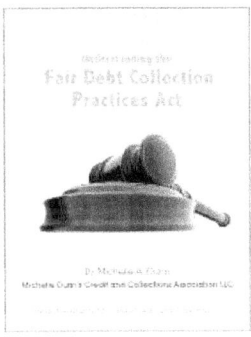

Books by Michelle are available in paperback and for your Kindle or any electronic device

Visit Michelle's blog www.Credit-and-Collections.com for more information to help you get paid, limit credit risk and make more money.